Where Does It Come From?

From Tree to Paper

by Avery Toolen

Bullfrog
Books

Ideas for Parents and Teachers

Bullfrog Books let children practice reading informational text at the earliest reading levels. Repetition, familiar words, and photo labels support early readers.

Before Reading

- Discuss the cover photo. What does it tell them?

- Look at the picture glossary together. Read and discuss the words.

Read the Book

- "Walk" through the book and look at the photos. Let the child ask questions. Point out the photo labels.

- Read the book to the child, or have him or her read independently.

After Reading

- Prompt the child to think more. Ask: How do you use paper? Have you ever thought about where it came from?

Bullfrog Books are published by Jump!
5357 Penn Avenue South
Minneapolis, MN 55419
www.jumplibrary.com

Copyright © 2022 Jump! International copyright reserved in all countries. No part of this book may be reproduced in any form without written permission from the publisher.

Library of Congress Cataloging-in-Publication Data

Names: Toolen, Avery, author.
Title: From tree to paper / by Avery Toolen.
Description: Minneapolis, MN: Jump!, [2022]
Series: Where does it come from? | Includes index.
Audience: Ages 5–8. | Audience: Grades K–1.
Identifiers: LCCN 2020047002 (print)
LCCN 2020047003 (ebook)
ISBN 9781645279853 (hardcover)
ISBN 9781645279860 (paperback)
ISBN 9781645279877 (ebook)
Subjects: LCSH: Papermaking—Juvenile literature.
Classification: LCC TS1105.5 .T67 2022 (print)
LCC TS1105.5 (ebook) | DDC 676—dc23
LC record available at https://lccn.loc.gov/2020047002
LC ebook record available at https://lccn.loc.gov/2020047003

Editor: Eliza Leahy
Designer: Michelle Sonnek

Photo Credits: Muzhik/Shutterstock, cover (left); Voronin76/Shutterstock, cover (right), 3; Georgii Shipin/Shutterstock, 1; Karen Struthers/Shutterstock, 4; Christopher Barrett/Shutterstock, 5; Sheryl Watson/Shutterstock, 6–7, 22tl; Shutterstock, 8, 9, 23tl; charobnica/Shutterstock, 10–11, 22tr; Marka/Getty, 12–13, 22mr, 23bl; Moreno Soppelsa/Shutterstock, 14–15; Kenneth Sponsler/Shutterstock, 16, 23br; Alamy, 17, 22br; zefart/Shutterstock, 18–19, 22bl, 23tr; Dragon Images/Shutterstock, 20–21, 22ml; Sanit Fuangnakhon/Shutterstock, 24.

Printed in the United States of America at Corporate Graphics in North Mankato, Minnesota.

Table of Contents

Pulp and Dry

Lee draws on paper.

Where does paper come from?

Trees!

Trees are cut down.

Logs go to a factory.

bark

A machine takes the bark off.

wood
chips

The wood is chopped.
It makes wood chips.

Water is added
to make pulp.

The pulp is cleaned.

pulp

Pulp goes in a machine.
It dries.
It makes paper sheets.

Sheets go on big reels. Wow!

reel

Next, paper is cut.

It is packaged.

It goes to stores.

We buy paper.
We write and
draw on it!

From Log to Notebook

How is wood made into paper that we use? Take a look!

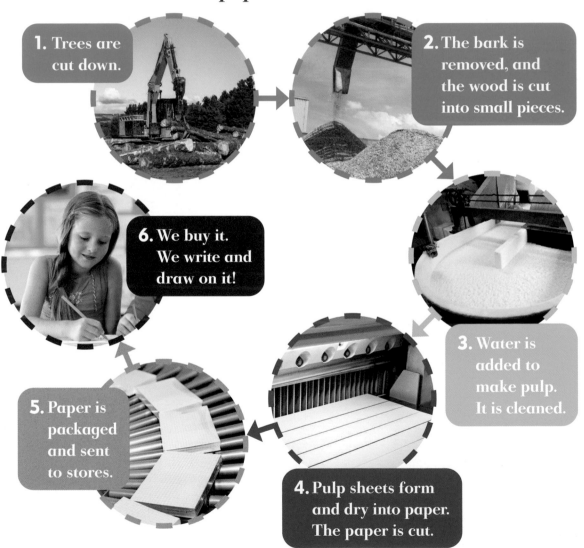

1. Trees are cut down.

2. The bark is removed, and the wood is cut into small pieces.

3. Water is added to make pulp. It is cleaned.

4. Pulp sheets form and dry into paper. The paper is cut.

5. Paper is packaged and sent to stores.

6. We buy it. We write and draw on it!

Picture Glossary

bark
The rough outer layer of a tree's trunk, roots, and branches.

packaged
Put in a container or wrapping.

pulp
A soft, wet substance made out of wood that is used to make paper.

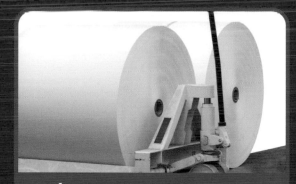

reels
Devices that can be turned in a circular motion to wind up and hold a flexible material.

Index

To Learn More

Finding more information is as easy as 1, 2, 3.

❶ Go to www.factsurfer.com

❷ Enter "fromtreetopaper" into the search box.

❸ Choose your book to see a list of websites.